Emily Post's Motor Manners
...the bluebooklet of traffic etiquette

Originally published in 1949
Republished by AGG Publishing 2013©

Cover photo by Dennis E. Horvath of a Marmon Sixteen 2013©

More photo artwork by Horvath available at
http://www.autogiftgarage.com/products/AutoGiftGarage-Automotive-Fine-Art.html

A Note on Emily Post's transcontinental journey by auto

By Terri Horvath

Before she became known as the premier expert on etiquette, Emily Post was already recognized as a writer. Her expertise and feminine outlook were called upon in 1915 for a transcontinental trip in the newfangled contraption known as the automobile. She accepted the challenge and submitted a series of articles on the journey to *Colliers*.

Accompanying her were her son Ned, who served as driver, and a cousin through marriage Alice Beadleston Post. Starting in New York City, they traveled along the Lincoln Highway, the country's first transcontinental road. Here they encountered some primitive road conditions. West of Chicago, the road was particularly deplorable. But, on they went, documenting every detail of the trip.

Prior to arriving in Chicago, she wrote "We had expected the scenery to be uninteresting. Instead no one with a spark of sentiment for his own country could remain long indifferent."

But west of Chicago, she had less than flattering descriptions. "An ugly, down-at-heels, uncomfortable hotel makes you think the same of the city. I do realize...it is a very distorted judgment that appraises a town by a few rooms in a hotel." Still, the well-bred socialite was delighted by people's welcoming reception time after time. The home-spun, all-out welcome by most people was the highlight of her tour, she recalled.

By the time she reached Santa Fe, NM, she became enthralled by the southwestern landscape. She was awed by the wide spaces and vivid colors of country once unknown to her. Travels abroad, she said, did not prepare her for the "wonders of the Southwest."

She reached San Francisco and San Diego in California 45 days after leaving New York City. The journey convinced her of the benefit of automotive travel.

Then in 1922 her landmark book on etiquette was published. By 1932, she had become a popular fixture on radio programs. Plus, her syndicated column was carried daily in about 200 newspapers.

She founded the Emily Post Institute, which carries on her work today, in 1942. Post continued her career until nearly 1960 when she died at the age of 87 years.

Motor Manners

Thanks. Millions of motor vehicle drivers and pedestrians will be grateful to Emily Post when they appreciate that greater courtesy will make driving and walking safer, more convenient and pleasant.

Bad manners are out of place anywhere. Because they lead to serious consequences—even casualties—in traffic, Emily Post, as the most eminent authority on good manners, has contributed her thinking in this booklet to enhance courteous relationships on the highways.

On behalf of the 1,000 organizations in the National and State Highway Users Conferences and their many millions of members, we wish to thank Mrs. Post and to present her "Motor Manners" to the American public.

Albert Bradley, Chairman
National Highway Users Conference, Inc.

Far too little traffic courtesy is shown on our highways. In fact, this lack of courtesy by highway users contributes not only to confusion and traffic congestion, but bad motor manners can all too often result in MURDER.

Behind the wheel of a car, men and women both whose behavior in all other circumstances is beyond reproach, become suddenly transformed into bad mannered autocrats. This inconsistency is certainly one of the unsolved mysteries of our time.

The driver, who tries to be considerate, becomes jittery when exposed to repeated experiences with rude drivers. This otherwise safe and well-mannered person, through induced impatience and irritability, may become "an accident going to happen."

When motor vehicles first appeared beginning of this century, it was the beginning of a new era of social behavior. New situations were thrust upon the "new motorist" for which no precedent had established proper manners. Horse and buggy etiquette was soon outdated and was not replaced. However, it was not until after World War I that automobiles became so popular that they could be counted by the millions and little by little became the unsolved highway problem of today.

Now with approximately forty million motor vehicles used so extensively for both business and pleasure we are all exposed many hours each week to this human problem in a relationship which was unknown to the generations of yesterday.

motor manners in their infancy

Bad traffic manners would seem to be due to the shortness of their existence. After all courtesy has been slowly developed through the ages and its precepts handed down from generation to generation. The automobile is still so new and has come upon our society so rapidly, that in one or two generations we have not completed the necessary code for our proper use of it.

safe driving rules must be obeyed

Primitive, irresponsible, discourteous and impatient behavior behind the wheel of an automobile has no place in society. Our legislators have attempted to establish safe driving rules in the motor vehicle laws. Upon close analysis of almost all our traffic laws one realizes that they are simply safe driving rules. Of course, this is reason enough for every person to comply with them. But the well-bred person will look deeper. He will see courtesy and well-mannered human conduct in practically every traffic rule.

For these reasons a gentleman will no more cheat a red light or stop sign than he would cheat in a game of cards. A courteous lady will not "scold" others raucously with her automobile horn any more than she would act like a "fishwife" at a party!

Courtesy in an automobile is always one's best assurance of safety.

Motor vehicle manufacturers have spared no expense in research and in engineering design to build safer cars, trucks and buses. Highway departments, the police, traffic engineers and many others strive to improve the safety of streets and highways. When all users of our highways show more courtesy and consideration for each other, the far reaching advantages of highway transportation will be advanced to a point where driving and walking can be a pleasant experience in a well-mannered society.

Since horse and buggy etiquette is too slow for today's highway transportation pace, the following questions and answers on traffic etiquette for the driving and walking public are presented to help reduce our woeful lack of motor manners. After all, courtesy can prevent property damage, injuries, suffering and death. Lack of it is unforgivable!

the golden rule

Q. How does the Golden Rule apply to traffic etiquette?

A. Doing unto others as you would have others do unto you is an opportunity offered every highway user many times each day. Only boorish drivers encountering heavy pedestrian traffic swear at it as though pedestrians have no right crossing the streets. Conversely, it is most bad tempered for pedestrians to pour their abuse on drivers. Many pedestrians are drivers who have parked their cars and pedestrians who are riding.

guides to safety

Q. What consistency can be noted between traffic rules, safety rules and good manners?

A. If you analyze traffic laws, you will find that almost every one is a safety rule. For example, right-of-way rules are designed to prevent conflicts at intersections. If you analyze further you will discover that almost every safety rule typifies some sort of good manners. One of the right-of-way rules requires that a vehicle about to enter an intersection must yield right-of-way to other vehicles already in the intersection. This logical rule, like many others, is simply in line with good manners—consideration for the rights of others. In other words, "first come, first served."

keep to the right

Q. Why should a polite driver keep to the right?

A. Keeping to the right is a recognized American highway custom. Therefore, it is well to develop the habit of staying on the right side of the road even when there are no other cars in sight.

entering a car

Q. Is it proper for the driver to get behind the wheel from the street side of the car?

A. This common practice is discourteous to other drivers. People who enter a car from the street side are actually being rude to other drivers. Either they force passing cars to stop and tie up other traffic, or they may cause drivers to swerve suddenly into another lane. Such thoughtlessness can lead to a collision between passing vehicles. Many drivers furthermore do not expect to encounter pedestrians mid-block or walking out from behind parked cars. In some cities, the law forbids this dangerous practice. Courtesy forbids it everywhere.

giving assistance

Q. Why is it good manners to help drivers in distress?

A. If drivers put themselves in the place of the motorist with the stalled car the answer is plain. The Golden Rule has always been key to all courtesy. A generous driver will assist friends or neighbors when their cars are stuck in snow or ice. It takes little time to give a stalled motorist a push when the battery is low. Going to the aid of travelers in distress has always been the mark of well-bred people. In fact, commercial drivers have often been called "gentlemen of the highway," because they so readily give their help to motorists in trouble.

stop lights

Q. Aren't hand signals for stopping unnecessary when all cars come equipped with stop lights?

A. No. The purpose of the hand signal to indicate a stop is to forewarn other motorists that you intend to stop. Your stop light does not operate until your brakes are applied. Often this is too late to warn the motorist following you, especially if it happens to be one of those rude drivers who follow so closely as to seem to be breathing down the back of your neck.

highway gentlemen

Q. Who are "Gentlemen of the Highway?"

A. Until now this term has been generally reserved to the good truck driver who demonstrates, by his conduct every day on the highway, that courtesy pays. Of course, there are other truck drivers who have not yet made this discovery for themselves and their employers. But, a "Gentleman of the Highway" can be anyone. The kind of vehicle a person drives is not important, whether new or old, high priced or low priced, commercial or private. It is _how_ a person drives. To be considered a lady or gentleman of the highway is becoming a mark of esteem these days. Your friends and family take pride in riding with you and it is a pleasure to meet you on the highway.

helping the police

Q. How will a courteous person cooperate with policemen?

A. By closely heeding traffic policemen's instructions, drivers and pedestrians can do much to make street traffic more orderly, After all, expediting traffic is the policeman's job, and his efficiency benefits the users of the streets. It is poor sportsmanship to display resentment to reasonable police signals. On the other hand, while many policemen today are trained to be courteous and are chosen for their intelligence among other qualities, there are still those who could mind their own manners better. These officers should realize constantly that they mold public opinion of visitors toward their cities. The same courteous attitude should be followed by drivers of emergency vehicles. While the public owes them the fullest cooperation in the granting of the right-of-way, emergency drivers should never abuse that privilege or use it except in actual emergencies. They should also realize that their siren does not give them license to be reckless.

speeding

Q. How does the courteous driver use his speedometer?

A. The speedometer is among the many safety devices built in cars. Only a traffic moron thinks that speedometers are provided to prove to friends how fast his car can go. Any one knows that any simpleton can hold an accelerator down. One of the best ways for passengers to judge the road etiquette of their drivers is by noticing the manner in which they adjust velocity to road conditions so that no emergency will catch them in a position where speed is out of control.

Q. What important considerations does a courteous driver give to controlling his speed?

A. The most important consideration is to drive as reasonable and prudent for the existing traffic environment. Courteous drivers adjust their speed to the density of the traffic which it is travelling; the type of road; the effect of weather on the pavement and on visibility; and the frequency of pedestrians, intersections, curves and hills. Finally, the best drivers slow down at night.

Q. Does courtesy require a driver to speed up when urged to hurry by a passenger?

A. Absolutely not. Hurrying through traffic shows little regard for the safety of others. Passengers reflect good manners when they do not urge their drivers to "step on it," to "beat the lights" or to commit any other unsafe practice that may lead to arrest or much worse, to casualty. Drivers and passengers alike should always remember that safety for all on the highway is paramount to anyone's personal urgency.

courtesy to passengers

Q. What driver courtesies add to passenger comforts?

A. A well-mannered driver will never frighten the passengers by careless or reckless maneuvering. Inattention to the road ahead; releasing the grip on the steering wheel to gesture or to light a cigarette, meanwhile allowing the car to wander; and breaking traffic rules are all signs of careless driving which disturb passengers. The obliging driver "host" will arrange for proper heating or ventilation for the comfort of his "guests." The accomplished driver automatically makes smooth starts and stops, not jerky ones.

courtesy to drivers

Q. What amenities should passengers show the driver?

A. Considerate passengers do nothing to distract their driver. Ceaseless chattering, arguing, crowding too many in the front seat, loud playing of the radio, are all examples of annoyances. The driver must be allowed to devote his entire effort and attention to the road. No other demands should be made of him. In fact, passengers can be politely helpful by assisting the driver in reading road maps and looking for road signs.

women drivers

Q. Why should no distinction be made between women in motoring manners?

A. While gallantry is expected of all gentlemen, on the highway women drivers lose the ready identity of their sex and simply become "another driver." Courteous drivers show full consideration for the safety and convenience of all "other drivers." In fact, split second decisions do not allow sufficient time to make a distinction nor does safety justify it. Only a pseudo-gentleman will make a show of chivalry to women drivers and then tangle bumpers in a bluffing match with a man driver.

pedestrian courtesy

Q. What are some of the reasons why drivers would "bend over backwards" to be courteous to pedestrians?

A. Responsible drivers realize that since they control the power to inflict injury, special precautions must be taken by them to avoid a casualty. Drivers with experience know that non-driving pedestrians do not realize how difficult it is to spot a pedestrian, to stop a car immediately, or to dodge suddenly in traffic. In addition, not all pedestrians a driver encounters can command the full capacity of their faculties. Considerate drivers know that the persons on foot may be, for example, bewildered, sick, crippled, deaf, blind or intoxicated.

Q. On which side of a highway is it correct to walk?

A. In the country, or where there are no sidewalks, pedestrians should walk on the left side of the road. This allows them to face vehicles which will pass nearest them. Drivers, on the other hand, should approach with caution less thoughtful pedestrians who are walking on the right hand side of the road with their backs toward an approaching car. At night, careful pedestrians carry a light or some white object. This helps the driver see them at a greater distance. This is courteous to the driver and plain common sense for the pedestrians.

Q. What courtesies should be shown in safety zones?

A. Mannerly pedestrians on a streetcar safety island during rush hours will be most cautious to avoid pushing others into either the car tracks or the roadway. Want of this civility is rowdyism and can be tragic. Pedestrians who climb over safety fences or barriers erected at such points, show childish behavior. Considerate drivers will not speed by these zones, frightening pedestrians or taking the risk of hitting an unwary one who at that moment decides to leave the platform or curb. In bad weather an accommodating motorist will give these pedestrians a better-than-even break to cross to the sidewalk. Never does a courteous driver allow his car to splash pedestrians.

Q. Why should pedestrians show courtesy to drivers?

A. Just as every well-mannered driver makes it clear to every other driver exactly what he is going to do, all well-mannered pedestrians will do their part to keep a driver from running the risk of killing them. Even if you don't care about protecting your own life, it is a terrible thing to make an innocent driver commit mayhem unwittingly. Therefore, courteous pedestrians refrain from appearing in the street where motorists do not expect to find them.

Q. What courtesy should a driver show at stop lights?

A. A courteous driver will always stop for a red light in a position that does not block the pedestrian crosswalk, and will always permit a pedestrian to finish crossing when he gets caught in the intersection by a change of lights. A well-mannered driver, who is about to make a turn through a pedestrian crosswalk, will proceed with utmost caution to enhance the safety of those on foot, remembering that they are crossing with a green light.

sharing rides

Q. Is the failure to pick up a pedestrian discourteous?

A. Just as a host does not welcome strangers into his home, a driver should be cautious taking strangers into his car. Tragic experiences warn owners against giving a stranger a ride. Therefore, no pedestrian should resent a driver's not stopping to pick him up. Friends should also realize that a driver might not recognize the identity of one who is walking. Many companies have strict rules against employees picking up "riders."

trucks on hills

Q. What courtesy can truck drivers show motorists?

A. An excellent example of highway courtesy and safety is the special instruction that many truck operators give their drivers requiring them to pull off the road for a few minutes if they happen to be holding up other vehicles on a steep hill. Drivers who make their living on the highway know that courtesy in sharing the road pays dividends.

window manners

Q. What "window manners" should be observed in a car?

A. Inconsiderate gestures from your car window can lead an unwary driver, approaching or following, into assuming these motions are hand signals. Neither passengers nor drivers should confuse other motorists by extending their hands or arms from car windows, flicking ashes from cigarettes, pointing at the scenery, or riding with their elbows out of the window and hands on the roof of the car. A courteous motorist never throws lighted cigarettes from a car window. They blow back or even fall and start roadside fires.

making turns

Q. What is the correct method of making turns?

A. Courteous drivers enter the proper lane sufficiently far in advance of a turn to avoid confusion occasioned by "jockeying for a position" near the turnoff. Right turns are made from the right had lane into the same lane of the cross street. Left turns should begin in the lane closest to the right of the center of the street, and courteous drivers turning left enter the corresponding lane on the cross street without cutting corners. Mannerly drivers signal their intentions to turn well in advance. They observe right-of-way rules at intersections and never straddle lanes prior to making a turn nor swing one way before turning the other. Greater caution and courtesy should be displayed in making left turns because drivers must cross other streams of traffic. Courteous drivers never block an intersection while waiting to turn, or joust with other cars or pedestrians for the right-of-way.

dimming lights

Q. Why should one always dim headlights at night?

A. Thoughtfulness of the comfort of the others requires that one always dims headlights when not to do so would cause painful annoyance to other drivers. State laws require the dimming of lights of the "driving beam" when meeting other cars at night on highways. Blinding another driver by a blaze of light is not only rude but dangerous and vicious. Drivers who courteously dim their lights first politely invite others to do the same. Don't overlook the fact that you can be the victim of a driver you "blind." If the full benefit of your dimming is to be realized, be sure that your headlights are properly pointed so that when they are dimmed no part of their beam will strike the eyes of on-coming drivers.

seating a lady

Q. Does courtesy require a gentleman to seat a lady first?

A. The age-old custom of a gentleman opening the door and assisting a lady into a vehicle is still in vogue. The modern independence of woman does not forbid this courtesy. When the car is parked on a busy street or thoroughfare, no lady expects a gentleman to help her into the front seat first and then walk around the car into traffic and climb in behind the wheel from the street side. Therefore, a courteous driver will, after assisting his passengers into the rear seat, excuse himself and slip into the driver's seat from the curb side ahead of other front seat passengers.

backseat driving

Q. Is "backseat driving" really in bad taste?

A. The backseat driver has been much maligned and often rightly so. The critical passenger can breed trouble in traffic by making a driver "jittery." This in turn upsets his driving judgment. There is, however, something to be said for any passenger who is obviously frightened. In fact, no sensible driver would resent being asked to drive more carefully.

courtesies in a car

Q. Should a gentleman who is driving light the cigarette of a lady beside him?

A. The answer is no! Safety is more important than chivalry. The driver of a car is not expected to light a passenger's cigarette, tune the radio, crank windows (other than his own) or do anything else that would momentarily divert his attention from the road, while trying to be helpful.

courtesy in parking

Q. What rude manners should be avoided in parking?

A. The driver who noses a car into a space about to be occupied by another shows impudent manners. Overtime parking is thievery from the standpoint of etiquette. Those who "store" their cars in limited parking places indicate their unwillingness to share their privilege to drive with others. Double parkers are in the same category. It is thoughtless to park in such a position that passengers are forced to squeeze their way past some curbside obstacle. Courteous drivers neither monopolize space for two parked cars, nor park so close that others are prevented from pulling out. In marked parking places considerate people stay within the lines. They are careful never to block someone else's driveway or a fire plug. Good manners and good sense dictate that vehicles be parked completely off the paved portion or rural highways if possible. On leaving a parking place the driver should give the proper signal and check to see that no other cars are coming.

Q. Why is it courteous to learn to park efficiently?

A. A driver's efficiency in parking is proof of the ability to control the vehicle with precision. Drivers are rude and selfish when they hold up other traffic while laboring to get into a parking place. They expose lack of skill as well as lack of manners. To display inept parking techniques is somewhat like a discordant amateur musician laboring through a poor performance to everyone's distress.

accident scenes

Q. What constitutes good manners at an accident scene?

A. Most state laws require that motorists stop and render assistance at scenes of accidents. The basest coward alive is the "hit-and run" driver. Drivers' reactions at emergency or accident scenes are certainly ones from which their passengers can judge their humane qualities. The considerate driver will give assistance to the limit of his or her ability and will see that medical care is provided if necessary. When coming upon a traffic accident scene already under control by the authorities drivers will, in good taste, continue on their way. Lingering adds to confusion which can limit the efficiency of those in charge. Only one having morbid curiosity stands by to stare at another's misfortune.

proper signals

Q. What correct signals will a courteous driver use?

A. No standard answer can be given concerning hand signals. Since the required method of hand signals varies among states, the correct answer is to follow the rules of the state in which you are driving at the time. Most states, however, have adopted uniform hand signals and more states can be expected to do so. This is a fine service to courtesy and safety. The use of mechanical signals provided by motor vehicle manufacturers is more convenient. The most important point is that courteous drivers always signal properly before stopping, turning, slowing down, or pulling out from a parking place. These courtesies take the guess work out of one driver determining what another will do and thus help prevent emergencies.

blind automobiles

Q. Why do courteous drivers go to the trouble of removing snow and ice from their cars?

A. In winter weather courteous drivers will remove ice or snow from all windows, including the rear one, as well as from the head and tail lights. Safety is at stake. Furthermore, no well-mannered person would require a passenger to ride in a blind car any more than he would require his guests to eat their dinner in the dark.

abuse of horn

Q. Is a loud horn a better warning than a standard one?

A. Trumpet horns—those penetrating signals designed for use on the open road—are as out of place when used in city driving as hobnail shoes in a ballroom. Another incivility is the unnecessary blowing of a horn in a traffic line when it can do no good and is merely annoying to others. People who would never dream of bawling a vocal protest will, at a moment's delay in traffic, blast away at every hesitancy of the car ahead.

Q. Should a driver warn pedestrians by blowing the horn?

A. If it is necessary in order to prevent an accident, the answer is yes. But no polite driver ever charges at an individual or a crowd of persons on foot, blowing the horn as if to blast them out of the way.

Q. What is the proper use of an automobile horn?

A. A courteous driver uses the horn as a warning only in emergencies, or, gently as polite signal. If more people realized that the horn, as the voice of the car, is in reality the voice of the driver, there would be less raucous thoughtlessness in its use.

Q. Should the horn be used to announce arrival or to call someone to the car?

A. No young man of good taste will announce his arrival to a lovely lady by standing at the curb outside her door and "yoo-hooing." Yet this is the identical offense which so many commit. Upon arriving by motor they sit at the wheel and blast away at the horn. A well-mannered visitor will alight and ring the doorbell.

traffic weavers

Q. Why is weaving in traffic bad manners?

A. Drivers who weave in and out of traffic betray either bad temper or disregard for other people. Both are serious breaches of etiquette. Weaving from one lane of traffic to another; constantly jockeying for a favorable position, causing sudden stops, near sideswipes and irritation among other drivers reminds one only of the behavior of certain barnyard animals at feeding time. Such road hogs fail to realize the risk they have taken; the position into which they have forced other innocent drivers; and, actually, that they themselves may be only several seconds closer to their destination for all this obstinate behavior. Often the confusion they cause may actually delay everybody, including themselves. Blocking others' paths by straddling two lanes, obstructing an intersection or nosing in and out is the abominable conduct of a glutton who forces his way to be first at the table. On the highway these vicious manners can result in manslaughter.

passing

Q. At what places on the road do well-behaved drivers refrain from passing?

A. The most dangerous places are on curves, hills or where the sight distance is insufficient for safe passing, or in an intersection or on railroad tracks. To do so is not only dangerous, it is frightening to others. A driver who will sometimes criticize a lady ahead of him in the theatre for wearing a big hat which blocks his view is often less worried about the adequacy of his sight distance on the highway. Other places where careful drivers never pass are on narrow bridges, wet streetcar tracks, on icy pavements or wherever other hazards exist.

slow drivers

Q. How can slow driving be discourteous?

A. To go too slowly is rude because it impedes the free flow of traffic. This is very irritating to other drivers who are trying to operate at reasonable speeds. This rudeness may even lead some to try to pass such a "snail" in an unsafe place. The courteous driver moves along at approximately the same speed of other vehicles on rural highways, parkways or wherever traffic is heavy, provided such speed is safe.

traffic lights

Q. What are the important courtesies between drivers at traffic lights?

A. Courteous drivers know that the amber light predicting a change in signals is for the purpose of "clearing the intersection." Only an impatient and thoughtless driver will use an amber light to jump the gun in starting. Only a reckless motorist will enter an intersection on the amber change light. It is unfair to other motorists to lag when the traffic light turns green and thereby hold up cars behind. Every driver knows that he must stop for a red light. A well-mannered driver will no more "cheat the lights" than cheat at cards.

school buses

Q. What courtesy should drivers display when encountering a stopped school bus?

A. While not all state laws require a full stop upon coming to a halted school bus, common sense and courtesy demand it. A cautious driver will not proceed until he has determined that it is absolutely safe and proper to do so. The driver who sneaks by stopped school buses because no policemen are around has only a slight resemblance to a naughty child misbehaving when not watched. What he really is exhibiting is barbaric behavior that can cause casualties to innocent persons.

children in the street

Q. What courtesy should drivers show children?

A. Experienced drivers know that children cannot always be held responsible for their actions. Lack of consideration for children in the street can result in manslaughter. All careful and polite motorists keep on the look-out for pre-school age youngsters who may dart into the street. Mannerly drivers will always slow down and proceed with caution in school zones. Every civil motorist will cooperate with school boy patrolmen as they go about their serious business of protecting their younger school mates. It should shame many grown-ups that school children are frequently their peers in pedestrian courtesy and manners.

right-of-way

Q. Why is the right-of-way only of the most important traffic courtesy rules?

A. It is important because these rules establish the priority of the movement of vehicles and pedestrians at intersections, driveways, in making left turns and wherever there are possibilities of conflicts. All right-of-way rules are evidences of good manners. But they are often misunderstood. Since right-of-way rules are not always consistent between different communities, the correct local mode must be accepted. It is a case of "doing as the Romans do." Stealing the right-of-way from someone else is offensive. Polite drivers never usurp another person's privilege. They are seldom in such a hurry that they can't pause for a courteous or friendly act.

drinking and driving

Q. Is it proper to drive after just one or two little drinks?

A. Not half enough emphasis is laid on preventing exhilarated, though far from drunken drivers from operating their cars. Their condition may cause them to take chances they would not think of taking when they have had nothing to drink. Can they adequately meet the many sudden traffic emergencies that arise? It is unnecessary to emphasize the menace of drunken drivers; certainly there is nothing to be said in their defense nor would good citizens want them to escape the full penalty of the law. Drunk drivers are the highway's deadliest menace. Drunk driving is heinous—criminal, but what many persons fail to realize is that the driver who may be classified as exhilarated also can be guilty of grave offenses. Nobody is immune to the affect of alcohol. Why then will any sane person drive while thus handicapped? It is a social obligation to keep inebriated persons out of the driver's seat.

Rude drivers

Q. Are rude drivers always rude persons elsewhere?

A. The point to be made—because so hard to understand—is that rude drivers often are, under other circumstances, perfectly well-behaved people. The man who tries to force his way ahead in a line of cars often would not think of trying to force himself ahead of others in a box office queue nor would he shove a fellow pedestrian off a sidewalk. If he accidentally did such a thing he probably would be mortified by his own rudeness. But, in his car, he is quite likely to swear roundly at his victim for getting in his way. Genuine manners are part of every gentleman—and lady—and are not removable.

the code of courtesy

Bad motoring manners can be murder. Just plain simple courtesy and consideration for others at all times will make the use of streets and highways safer, more efficient and more pleasurable. Here is a "Code of Courtesy" that can be followed by all would be well-mannered drivers and pedestrians.

1. A well-mannered driver will share the road, never usurping the right-of-way from other vehicles or pedestrians.

2. A well-behaved driver uses his horn as a warning device in emergencies and never as a bad-tempered voice to threaten or scold.

3. An honorable man or woman would no more cheat traffic regulations than cheat at games or in sports.

4. Courteous pedestrians will cross busy streets at intersections, respect traffic lights and avoid darting out from behind parked vehicles.

5. An obliging driver will never fail to dim his lights when meeting other cars in the dark.

6. Well-bred people, whether drivers or passengers, are just as considerate of each other as are hosts and guests in a drawing room.

7. An accommodating driver parks his car so as not to interfere with the use of other parking spaces or with the movement of other vehicles.

8. Orderly drivers always keep to the right, except when using the proper lane for turning or passing.

9. A courteous driver never fails to signal his intentions to stop, turn or pull out.

10. Considerate persons always drive at speeds which are reasonable and prudent, considering traffic, road and weather conditions.

11. One who has any consideration for the safety of others will refrain from driving when physically exhausted.

12. Kindly persons never show curiosity at the scene of an accident and always give any assistance that may be passable.

Books focused on automotive history by Dennis E. Horvath and Terri Horvath

Indiana Cars: A history of the automobile in Indiana

Hoosier Tour: A 1913 Indiana to Pacific Tour

93 Tips for Buying a Collectible Car

Cruise-in Crosswords and Word Jumbles

Cruise-in Crosswords and Word Jumbles 2

More information about their books is available at http://www.autogiftgarage.com/bookstore/AutoGiftGarage-Bookstore.html

Made in the USA
Columbia, SC
23 March 2023